At Night

by **Barrie Wade** and **Tomislav Zlatic**

W
FRANKLIN WATTS
LONDON•SYDNEY

At night, the stars come out.

I can see them
from my window.

At night, the moon comes out.

I can see it
from my window.

5

At night, the moths come out.

I can see them
from my window.

7

At night, the mouse comes out.

8

I can see it run in my garden.

At night, the bats come out.

Here they come!

10

They like to fly
over my garden.

At night, the cats come out.

They like to play
in my garden.

At night, the owl comes out.

It sits in the tall tree

and hoots.

At night, the fox comes out.
I can see it digging
for beetles.

At night, I read
in my bed.

I love the animals at night!

AT NIGHT

19

Story trail

Start at the beginning of the story trail. Ask your child to retell the story in their own words, pointing to each picture in turn to recall the sequence of events.

Start

Independent Reading

This series is designed to provide an opportunity for your child to read on their own. These notes are written for you to help your child choose a book and to read it independently.

In school, your child's teacher will often be using reading books which have been banded to support the process of learning to read. Use the book band colour your child is reading in school to help you make a good choice. *At Night* is a good choice for children reading at Blue Band in their classroom to read independently.

The aim of independent reading is to read this book with ease, so that your child enjoys the story and relates it to their own experiences.

About the book

This story is set at night time. Looking out of her window, a young girl can see animals and insects as they come out to play at night.

Before reading

Help your child to learn how to make good choices by asking: "Why did you choose this book? Why do you think you will enjoy it?" Look at the cover together and ask: "What do you think the story will be about?" Support your child to think of what they already know about the story context. Read the title aloud and ask: "What can the girl see from her window?" How do you know it is night time?" Remind your child that they can try to sound out the letters to make a word if they get stuck.

Decide together whether your child will read the story independently or read it aloud to you. When books are short, as at Blue Band, your child may wish to do both!

During reading

If reading aloud, support your child if they hesitate or ask for help by telling the word. Remind your child of what they know and what they can do independently.

If reading to themselves, remind your child that they can come and ask for your help if stuck.

After reading

Use the story trail to encourage your child to retell the story in the right sequence, in their own words.

Support comprehension by asking your child to tell you about the story.

Give your child a chance to respond to the story: "Did you have a favourite part? Help your child think about the messages in the book that go beyond the story and ask: "Do you think the girl likes the night? Why/Why Not?"

Extending learning

In the classroom, your child's teacher may be reinforcing punctuation and how it informs the way we group words in sentences. Find the exclamation marks and ask your child to think about the expression they use for exclamations. (see page 10 and page 18). Some sentences in this story carry on over two lines, but it is important to reinforce the sentence ends with a full stop rather than a line break and keep reading until the full stops.

Franklin Watts
First published in Great Britain in 2017
by The Watts Publishing Group

Series Editors: Jackie Hamley and Melanie Palmer
Series Advisors: Dr Sue Bodman and Glen Franklin
Series Designer: Peter Scoulding

A CIP catalogue record for this book is
available from the British Library.

ISBN 978 1 4451 5477 0 (hbk)
ISBN 978 1 4451 5478 7 (pbk)
ISBN 978 1 4451 6089 4 (library ebook)

Printed in China

Franklin Watts
An imprint of
Hachette Children's Group
Part of The Watts Publishing Group
Carmelite House
50 Victoria Embankment
London EC4Y 0DZ

An Hachette UK Company
www.hachette.co.uk

www.franklinwatts.co.uk

For Ada – B.W.